*The*

POEMS

# Forgotten

GOLD WAKE

# *World*

NICK COURTRIGHT

Colophon: set in Aileron Thin, Pinyon Script, and Athelas

Written for 2021 by Nick Courtright
Published by Gold Wake Press

All author proceeds from this book are donated to charity;
please see the acknowledgments for more information

The contents of this book may be distributed freely

Other Gold Wake Press books by Nick Courtright:
*Let There Be Light* (2014) and *Punchline* (2012)

THE FORGOTTEN WORLD

# Contents


*Forgotten*    1

Facing Mecca    3

I Cannot Enter the Mosque    5

Clear Blue Sky    7

The Story of the Rug (You Can See in My Kitchen)    8

$8 "Nikes"    9

Waiting for the River    10

Chapel    12

Before Falling Out of Love    13

Frida Kahlo Atop the Pyramid of the Sun    15

Falling Out of Love    16

American Idiot    17

Altitude Sickness    18

I Should Stop Talking about Darkness    19

Forever Young    20

The Heights of Machu Picchu    21

*Forgotten*    25

Airplane to Bangkok    27

Inside Everyone is a Skull    29

Inside Everyone is a Wallet    31

The Last Samurai    33

A Matter of Scale     35

Losing One's Mind at Westminster Abbey and Notre
    Dame feat. Vincent Van Gogh     36

You—Zombie     41

Venus     42

Notice the Hills     44

Good King Wenceslas     45

Nostalgia for a Distant Future     46

Dracula's Last Day     47

The Italians Have It Right     48

Where You Are Going Is What You Are     51

*Forgotten*     53

Homecoming     55

My Mother Shaving Her Legs     56

All You Know on Earth and All You Need to Know     57

Oblique Letter to Young Son as He Confronts
    Adolescent Loneliness for the First Time     59

Sick Child as Hailstorm     61

Apples     63

The Next Generation     65

We Cannot Leave the House     67

When at the End of One Thing and at the Beginning
    of Another     68

Conclusion     71

To Keep Us Warm     72

# Forgotten

MOROCCO
KENYA
MEXICO
ECUADOR
PERU

# Facing Mecca

The call to prayer
reminds me of all I am not,

my heritage like gum
on a Walmart parking lot.

It calls through the evening,
the sun a memory

and the terrace a plateau
for my son's future test scores.

It calls through the evening
and elsewhere a monkey

on its chain backflips
for dirhams, and a cobra

dances its sultry terror
to the music of an instrument

I cannot name. What difference
would it make if I am clipped

by a motorbike, if I cannot smile
at an old woman, her niqab

concealing what it is about her
that I wish to know? If I gave in

to what I want, what sort
of tiled mosaic would I be,

flattened against a world
I will soon cease to remember?

Now I am still, I am still, I am
on the terrace and the call calls

from every direction.
Do I pray? I try, but I can't.

# I Cannot Enter the Mosque

Inside a body bones are wet.
They are not the sun-

cooked whiteness of the forever-
dry the way ancient deserts like.

They are wet, they shine like teeth
growing from a jackal's jaw,

ready to please. They are not
battling dehydration

in the 14th century,
the sun an egg yolk in the sky.

Wet bones, wet bones,
that's what your body holds.

I want to atone for all
I've not done, and for nothing

I have, the moon
like a flag in the black space,

a scimitar seen beneath
a cloak, the air a mosquito.

When irreligious
you can only go some places,

like bars, or houses, or heaven.
But I can't go here, what with

my white—. There is no funeral
that will change any of this,

there is no ritual
that will take that broken egg

and make it, again,
in its mother's nest, whole.

# Clear Blue Sky

I thought I was the one

who made the clouds

disappear, my eyes closing

like the beak of a bird.

It wasn't me, it was just

a night on which

the moon didn't shine,

so busy was the moon

reflecting how

different it could have been,

how like a sun, how

like a father.

# The Story of the Rug
## (You Can See in My Kitchen)

When he tells you his friendship
is not about money, it is about the heart,
that we are brothers now,

do you believe? He is not your brother.
He wants to sell you a rug,
he wants to sell you all of the rugs,

they are of the finest camel hair,
you can picture the camels'
long tongues, your life piled high with rugs.

So of course you buy,
because there is no not buying,
not when you are a coward.

You can give the rug away
but it will never leave you,
because you are no one's brother,

and because that would mean you belong,
just like the puddle
beneath a donkey's hoof.

# $8 "Nikes"

To be the largest city in the world
in the 12th century
is to stay in the 12th century,
all the improper gods of light whimpering
your name in the shouting dark.

There are plenty of languages to hear
but none of them do you speak
and that's again why this heavenly ball
is so big and my understanding of it
so failed by indifference:

you can get all the counterfeit goods
you want, or buy 45 spices
from a stoop-shouldered fellow's brother,
but it won't make the sweat on your back
any different from the sweat on his.

Could I say I am lost, that I can't read
the star charts, that all the satellite dishes
will one day be overflowing
with mint tea? The ocean is muted
by the jetties it slaps, the spray

shooting and tumbling like soldiers
and gymnasts, respectively.
One more café au lait should do the trick,
because then I will never sleep again,
which means never again will I wake.

# Waiting for the River

I want to write a book about the recent past

About the world you thought you were that is no longer the
world

It will include the unmasked faces of others

It will include something about power but I'm not sure how

It will include feeling alone and separate from your beloved

It will include ample guilt because that is earned

Maybe it will include an airplane

We seemed to like those

In the end it's all ephemera

Consciousness is neither harmed nor improved by what it
knows

The stock market and the universe are the same

We have ever-increasingly sophisticated ways of talking
about them though they are fundamentally impossible
to understand

The graveyard's full of people we couldn't do without

The graveyard's full of people without whom we couldn't do

Eventually I'll hide in my home not because I want to but
because I have to

So it goes

Here's my hand

I've got king high and all the hope in the world

# Chapel

In the rooms of the holy places
crying may be the only appropriate behavior.

Anything less and you are not doing it right.

Anything more and you have forgotten your role.

We are all beggars reaching for the cup of sadness,

when stillness would have our guitar case
full of gold coins and letters from heaven.

At some point all things must come to an end,
say those who believe in endings.

All I know is what I've been brought up to fear—

the burial we will endure
is not as important as the belief that we are dead.

# Before Falling Out of Love

I couldn't really make sense
of my happiness. There were zebras
in the distance and when
one turned beside the other
I could not tell where one began
and the other was also a zebra.
Weather was not alone and neither was I
though in both cases the situation
was temporary. You were there
and I couldn't make sense of it.
You wore a scarf and I wore a scarf
and if we got out of the vehicle
someone would probably die
so we stayed in the vehicle. They say
elephants have excellent memories
so if I came back to wander Tsavo
would they remember me?
Would they remember a man
in the time before the man
made decisions? Under a tree
a warthog tries to hold its ground
against five large hornbills
and then oh well the warthog
can't hold its ground. Now
it's the one cooking in the sun.
And the giraffe looks like a damn fool
when it tries to enjoy the waterhole.
It has to spread its legs so far apart
and while we fuck I think
"wow we're fucking in Africa." Zebras
are just too crazy to domesticate,
says Moses, and I trust him
more than I trust Muhammad, who lights
the joint, though I suppose

that when it comes down to it
I trust Muhammad too, and also Mustafeh
and Swale. Eventually I'll be back
in my bed in America after having
set my family on fire and outside
the storm rattles its chains
and my windows and before I know it
that too will be just a memory.

# Frida Kahlo Atop the Pyramid of the Sun

What can we make of our relationship
to the past, how Frida couldn't leave
her wounds behind, the failing leg
she'd one day lose, the uterus
pierced in a street car accident?
When she left Diego she became Las Dos

Fridas, and like this we betray the dreamers
we once were, our youths looming expired
as pyramids, great constructions abandoned
by time. Human beings are just another
in a long list of primates who have eaten
what they could until they couldn't.

There's no way to escape, no staring
into the eclipse the priests rightly predicted,
no amount of hand-carved obsidian
to hang around our necks as a talisman.
All the temples at Teotihuacan are sublime,
all the fields on which blood has pooled.

Frida, blazing, glorious, with her wound
surely could not climb that pyramid,
and now here I am, a spy in her bedroom.
I see her things, the dresses she wore,
the mirrors in which she became real. Now
when I look at the sun all I see is black.

# Falling Out of Love

The flame moves in on the house this weekend,
the clever box and its faux wood flooring
and whitewash cabinets, too many white
cabinets, the flame moving in and through,

the flame brandishing its sad ancient dance
of romance and boyish extravagance,
putting its whole fist into its orange mouth
and through the thin wall and ceiling again,

past the kitchen, past the bathroom fixture
tottering like a flame, flame inhaling
and exhaling its mad animal breath,
curious flame flattening its belly

to the foyer floor, flame hanging like meat
from the rafters, flame popping the windows
like glass balloons as so much that has passed
passes and moves through this fickle night...what

full force is in effect when the house bows,
when smoke makes its dim drawings, when the blinds
nod their heads as another ceiling fan
curls its wooden petals like a flower?

# American Idiot

I see a pack of stray dogs
chase a tourist down the street
and as he swats at them
the rest of South America looks on, amused.

My mere existence, too, is comical. Orwell
in "Shooting an Elephant" remarked
that a colonist is always in a battle
not to be laughed at and now for the first time

I truly understand that. And Orwell,
with the brown faces staring him down,
what did he do, even though he didn't want to?
He shot the elephant. So I can lose

my passport and get rained on
and fail to bring the toucan into the sight
of my binoculars, while Irman makes it look so easy.
I can run sweating like a fool sweats

in search of something I don't know what
but regardless the role of every white man in this world
is to shut up and take it
because so much of this bed you for yourself have made.

# Altitude Sickness

I was scared above Ecuador
as the world splits here or comes together
and I am split here but with nothing else
do I come together. I find myself
in another church while outside
it thunders emotionally and the rain
did seem to wreck the protest in the square
that seemed more about eating ice cream
than anger at the intractability
of economic injustice.
This church is so gold it's hard to look at
because what conquest was required
to deliver to the Catholics
what like so much did not belong to them.
This is South America, not Rome.
I was afraid. Of Spanish, of aloneness, of brown
pure like chocolate or coffee
against the awfulness that is white.
A small child wanders down the center aisle
and falls on her face
as so many statues of Mary look on
in irrevocable indifference. I think of my father
and how I did not love him enough
when his parents died and how someday
I will pay for this. The house his parents lived in
for fifty years sits empty, their village
shuddering among the strip mines.
All the while, I watch from afar. In Quito
I am above 9000 feet and this means
I am atypically close to heaven.
It also means there's not enough oxygen.

# I Should Stop Talking about Darkness

It is somehow surprising when in a rainforest
it begins to rain. The sky becomes a sieve
and the Swiss man you just met

whose tan glistens like bread
finishes his cigarette by a waterfall
and complains about his Peruvian girlfriend

who is self-conscious about her bathing suit
and this is proof one place
is just like any other place.

Sure, the rustic waterslide into the rushing river
is a health hazard in violation of sanity
but the pure act of its existence

is a miracle, like the flowers, the flowers,
the flowers. Later, as part of a ceremony
a parade of teenage boys in blackface

parades down the dusty avenida
and it is unclear how I am supposed to feel
about this. In time with the music

the boys scrape their machetes
against the cobblestone and the sound it makes
is like reading Braille with broken fingers.

# Forever Young

I buy drugs off the street in Lima and use them
with someone whose teeth are very poor

but who speaks some English
and a man who claims his name is Tony Montana.

At some point I'm going to have to take
my decisions more seriously, but not yet. It is not time.

In Latin America they take Mother's Day
much more seriously, unlike my decisions.

They have signs for it in parks where people act out
in a variety of ways: dressing as clowns

and feating impressively with their bodies; swinging
like a child because you are a child in a swing;

getting faded on a blanket in the complacency
of parenthood. On Día de las Madres

police officers in the plaza grande give roses to mothers
they spot in the throng, or drink tea at a table

beneath the president's palace. I want to feel safe
but how could I? Everywhere here I am a mark.

Because I should be. I like generations of colonists
before me are vectors for crime.

# The Heights of Machu Picchu

1. Paparazzi

Here at Machu Picchu
it is exactly as you'd expect.
Beautiful, impressive, it will be all the photos say it will be.
How many photos of Machu Picchu is enough, I wonder
as I take a photo of Machu Picchu.
What a location! The Inca had ambition
and then they died. But the Inca were just the kings;
the people were Quechua.
They may or may not have had ambition
and then they died. The sounds of a weedwhacker
disrupt the vigil for all those dead
being kept by no one. I am a spoiled American
who is a voyeur on the heritage of those
who have heritage. A fly bites my ankle. A flock of tourists
follows two camelids like paparazzi
and I say camelid because I don't feel 100% certain
saying they are llamas and not alpacas
though I'm pretty sure they are llamas. I looked at a chart.
I wonder how to lend meaning to my life.
At Machu Picchu the bus that takes people to Machu Picchu
contributes to erosion that will end Machu Picchu.
Both llamas and alpacas know this to be true.
Every single person on this earth is just bumbling along.

2. Physics

Beneath the ruins of Ollantaytambo I pet an alpaca

beside the rushing water and consider aloneness but not
    loneliness.

Beneath the ruins of Ollantaytambo I consider the past and
    eat an alpaca.

Beneath the ruins of Ollantaytambo I think of chocolate and
    how the Mayans

never lived to see their discovery grace the salons of France.

Beneath the ruins I tire of the sun.

Beneath the ruins of Ollantaytambo I can't spare the change,

my calves on fire from too many mountains, my future a
    nest of confusion.

Beneath the ruins I wonder about ruins, and forsake my
    privilege.

Beneath the ruins of Ollantaytambo I turn my back.

Beneath the ruins I taste the chocolate, and the coffee, and
    the coca,

and scratch an alpaca's ear, and am the vaporous periphery
    of a universe that does not exist.

3. The Second Amendment

In Peru there seems to be an affinity
for 80s American easy listening music,
as confirmed by the passionate calm of the speakers
singing "Sexual Healing" as I wait
for a three-dollar colectivo to Cusco, the Inca capital.

And I wait, and wait, and then we are off
on our mission to death, to curse the name of Pizarro
in the name of Pachacuti and I am about done
being a tourist in this life. My conversations are broken
and as usual there are too many

white people around. So let's discuss
El Señor de los Temblores, the black Christ
of the Earthquakes who is paraded through the streets
like that army of middle school kids you saw
in ridiculous military march and isn't it something

that while I'm here there's another school shooting
in America while on this southern continent
a hot shower may be tough to come by, and you can't
drink from the faucet, and stray animals
argue with each other in the streets, but I do not

fear guns. Guns in the trees, guns in the sewers,
guns in your hands, guns in your face.
Here instead in the town plaza they do ceremonial dances.
Their clothes are bright. They are unarmed.
And then I go home. And then I go home.

Where there are no toucans except on cereal boxes,
and the dogs and cats are pets or will be or will not exist,
where I can understand what everyone is saying,
at least to the extent that anyone can ever understand
what anyone is saying. The tapwater will be drinkable;

the shower water will be hot. The water water will water
but not quite in the same way as it does
when it pours from a 400-year-old mountaintop fountain,
its engineers vanquished in a hail of superior weaponry.
At home more people will have guns, this is sure,

but I will worry less about having my camera stolen.
My neighbors may be shot in their home
but I will be safe in mine. What were those children doing
goose-stepping in the marketplace of Cusco?
Why didn't Atahualpa win? Why didn't he

drive the Spanish back to their boats?
Why couldn't the Temple of the Sun at Qorikancha resist
having the Church of Santo Domingo built atop it?
For whichever animal we have put to sleep
we have waken another to take its place.

# *Forgotten*


THAILAND
CAMBODIA
JAPAN
ENGLAND
FRANCE
THE NETHERLANDS
HUNGARY
CZECHIA
ITALY

# Airplane to Bangkok

The man next to me on the airplane is looking at a magazine
    full of photographs of children kneeling next to deer
    carcasses

His headphones barely conceal that he is listening to the
    Jimmy Buffett classic "Cheeseburger in Paradise"

He just farted

The row behind me is drunk and getting drunker

Their third round just served up

The flight attendant

Thirty years older and thirsty for popularity

Jokes with them

It is 8 a.m.

It is 8 a.m.

Even earlier there was the aggressively elderly woman in the
    San Francisco airport

She did not smile at me when I smiled at her

Her fingers were twisted like the branches of desert trees

When she stood up she gasped with surprise that she could

On the plane the stewardess is brusque and pale

She thrusts ice cream at customers as if they are prisoners

The in-flight movie features a punishingly long sequence in
    which a ship is tossed about by a violent sea

It really is a very long sequence

The airplane waves in its turbulence

The airplane waves in its turbulence

At the end of this in-flight movie

Which I am not watching

A man from the ship returns to his fiancée after having
    endured tremendous terror

She embraces him with undivided love

As he

Elsewhere

Stares into the distance

# Inside Everyone is a Skull

Cambodia is full of too much poverty

Gasoline is sold out of old liquor bottles

Children are not in school

Trash is everywhere

A monkey pulls over the rope railing protecting a priceless
    work of stone-carved temple art

The art depicts the ascension to the throne of Suryavarman

    a great king who was probably an asshole

    and a nearby fresco shows the churning of the sea of
    milk

    in which good and evil play cosmic tug of war using a
    large snake wrapped around a mountain

It sounds absurd when you put it like that

It also sounds absurd to drink the blood of someone who
    died two thousand years ago

It also sounds absurd to believe in telescopes

There is no way to put Cambodia into words

Less than forty years ago more than two million people died
    there from starvation and execution at the hand of a
    ruthless dictator

In a memorial no one visits skulls are stacked high behind
    glass

Literally they are stacked high

No one knows who belongs to these skulls

People responsible for this go unprosecuted today

But it's a new day

A monkey pulls over the rope railing protecting a priceless
    work of stone-carved temple art

# Inside Everyone is a Wallet

The Tokyo airport is like Vegas

But with whiskey samples and free wi-fi

I wander as a fool would wander and then head for sushi

I translate all of the yen and it is too much to think about

When I speak English I can see the pain in the faces of those
    I am speaking to even though they too speak English

I cannot even drink my drink properly

Nearby

A man debates whether to eat his illegal prescription drugs

Smuggle them

Or throw them away

This is a difficult decision

Soon after I hear a man with no legs say "you can't let anger
    be your guide

    it will just destroy you"

This is in the United Lounge

The United Lounge for the wealthy and privileged

It has its own complimentary beer dispenser as well as a
    ragged array of liquor bottles in the corner of the
    counter

It's difficult to decline such opportunity

As if that opulence weren't enough to make anyone feel
    awful

There's an elevator with golden sheen going up to a room
    reserved for the Global First Class

Who is up there

# The Last Samurai

In Japanese I never know where to put the stresses.
Vowels just get swallowed into nothing.
They are like dreams anyone could have

of ever understanding anyone else.
To have been among the neon or gaslight
and not like an American among the dandelions

there would be something exotic in the otherness
of perpetual loneliness, to be a candy
in the hand of a child or smushed as a human body

on the subway at Shinjuku, where the dress is professional
and there has never been a room more full and more quiet
than this one rushing like death

meters beneath the pattering sidewalks
of spotless Tokyo where it is never dangerous
even though it is so very bright and so very full.

When the sushi comes to you on its conveyor belt
of convenience and leisure, take what you want
because here the manners are so

sublimely as they are, like cherry blossoms
in a park, but months out of bloom, no blossoms at all,
what does it all amount to other than yen

and the sightless unstarred night
about the metropolis hovering like a katana, sharp
as a katana, grasped and sharp hovering desperation

like a katana, do it, take what you want,
it's just a heap of opportunity
downed like warm sake while sitting on a tatami mat

at a ryokan as the onsen billows its steam
against the mirror in which you could see yourself
if only you could be seen. But let's be honest here

for once: you can't be seen, because no one can be seen.

# A Matter of Scale

From far enough away
everything looks just about the same—
for example, the big map of the cosmos

a ten year old
has on his wall
likely won't require much updating in his lifetime

and in that
there's solace and something horrible:
all he'll ever do is small,

and though it may be remembered, it'll only be for a while.
See, even the ancient ancients
and all the sea-parting Moseses of history

and their pharaoh brethren
and the great monkey grandfather
whose works are etched in mud

we've yet to uncover, their memory as great and lasting
as it seems would be a miracle
if it made it past the sun's expiration.  Which nears.

# Losing One's Mind at Westminster Abbey and Notre Dame feat. Vincent Van Gogh

I. Transubstantiation

When you go to Westminster Abbey and take communion
this is the apex of sin. Or is it
the confession you needed, here
where Edward the Confessor's resting place
is too fragile to be trod upon by tourists?
What does it mean that I'm going to hell? Nothing:
Spenser's tomb says he awaits the Second Coming
and this is proof all we writers put ourselves
in compromising positions. Chaucer
was buried here not because *Canterbury*
but because he was a good civil servant. Even so long ago
being a writer was secondary to being
what you really are—part of the show.
Among all these dead I remember that we all die.
And the voice of the woman administering the Eucharist—
is she priest, pastor, minister, the guide says President—
her voice is glorious, as is her unbending
delivery of the rites you only imagine
she takes to be true. When she says The Body of Christ,
looking you in the eye, and you—I mean I—
say amen and accept what she gives
this is the exact moment something breaks,
and when her assistant, the staff-wielder, I do not know
the terms of the ceremony, says The Blood of Christ,
and I say amen, all I can think
are two things: I have not yet finished eating this body,
and I hope the blood does not spill down my chin.
And then I drink, and fast, too fast, I have done this thing,
I have made sacred what was sacred, I have made
profane what was profane, and the biggest shame
is that I have to get up. I have to walk,

the service is over, we are exiting the pews and shaking
hands and there are more
tombs to see, now that I have finished seeing my own.

2. Happy New Year

At Notre Dame I debated for three minutes
whether to enter the prayer-only section.
Immediately upon sitting I wept, saying
God, please help me. Later
I took my largest bite of duck just as I was passed
by a beautiful teen, who said to me: *bonne année.*
This, too, is a symbol of mortality. It's true
I cried a bit while seated in the prayer-only section
at Notre Dame Cathedral in Paris
asking God for help, but what did you do today?
In a bar named after Napoleon
I order the duck which I shouldn't have
and struggle with language and have epiphanies
that evaporate as soon as they arrive.
I second-guess my syntax, my sequencing
of grammatically interchangeable phrases,
and with good reason. Then I'm back to wandering
through my mind—I really have to get that thing
under control. Is that my resolution?
Yes, but I know goalsetting doesn't work.
I read this in a book. So what to do?
Where are my friends? Van Gogh, what was wrong?
I see the struggle in you. At Musée D'Orsay
I in trouble with myself came to you twice.
The you of the last self-portrait (1890),
or at least it's the one that should be last,
or at any other point on your journey. Your eyes
sparkle but disconcertedly. Later I'd weep
in a church and take a bite that was too large.

3. Insanity

*What is wrong right now* Eckhart Tolle asks and I say
*what is not.* There is oxygen here,
and a temperature at least somewhat compatible
with human life. This Americano
given to me by a skipping woman in London
is perfectly reasonable in its disposition. Every day
I wake up and my eyes and ears are functional, my glasses
are not too far to reach, I don't even have to take off
the covers. The shower water is hot, though
at first I couldn't find the next roll of toilet paper,
but then I looked behind the towels and voila, there it was.
The towels were red. This is London.
The buses are red and might run you over—
they are coming from the wrong direction. I cried
at the Venus de Milo and I cried begging
God for help at Notre Dame and I cried
for my grandparents at Westminster Abbey, where I sinned,
how awful it is what I've done. But none
of these things are right now, outside of my mind.
Right now is people eating mediocre British food.
Right now it's cold air coming through the door,
and a splash of panic. What is a psychic break?
What is a nervous breakdown? Confession:
I took the holy sacrament without belief. But this is just
a matter of aesthetics. There is no more moral wrong here
than what I have had imposed on me
by my personal history as a person living
in a world of human culture. I am the man at the end
of *Seize the Day*, weeping with deliverance.
Be patient. This is the biggest lesson I've forgotten. So what
if I stay up all night, so what if what
all these other people think is morning
is actually night? So what if it's cold pissing in the weeds
in a neighborhood at 6 AM and no one will remember
except the objective arbiter who does not exist?
You've done this to me before.
This is like the life of Van Gogh: the gradual
extinction of hope, seen in the photograph

with his back turned to the camera, seen face to face
time and time again as what becomes
more beautiful becomes more damaged.
It is cold outside. It is so very cold. I turn 37 this year.
Whitman said I now 37 years old in perfect health begin
and so was born Song of Myself.
By his mid 50s he had been leveled by a stroke
and saw the limbs of the Civil War
drop horribly into pails and the lightness of his work
was never quite the same. And at 37 Van Gogh
shot himself in the chest and died two days later,
or maybe he was shot, some now claim.
Before this, though, he said I want to be known
as the painter of sunflowers. In this way he succeeded.
In this way could I ever be so lucky?
In those paintings of sunflowers, though, some are dead.
Near the end of his days he painted looking out the window
of his room at the asylum, through the bars.

# You—Zombie

You—*zombie*—felt a century passing
and you loved it, having seen what there was
to see, as in your state you saw only
what would elicit continuation.

You had to debate what was important
to you: the television, the photo
albums, the incontinent terrier?
The heart of your son, the heart of your mom,

the hearts of strangers frightened in the night?
Despite illness, it remained possible
to engineer complex analogies
regarding the fundamental nature

of the human condition.  A fact, though,
was that even on your very best days
you yearned to eat all the flesh you could find
though you'd long ago recognized that's all

it was: just flesh.  Not life.  Not truth.  Not love.
In the village of zombies we zombies
pull limbs from the living because we are
lonely, because it is what we must do.

# Venus

Everyone knows about your arms.
Fewer know of the toe you are missing, the loss
that is Art, the beauty that cannot be kept.
Likewise, no one knows if the end of "Ode

on a Grecian Urn" makes the poem or destroys it.
All around you, Venus, are humans, and they capture
you in photos, they coil around you in lumps,
they want to be close to you, but mostly

for a picture they won't look at more than three times.
But it's okay: I did it too. This is what we are,
not the subtle definition of your abdomen,
not the folds of gown hiding from us

what we really want to see. Milo, where you were found,
means apple, which you were holding,
and there is the coolness of your skin, the soft hump
of your breasts, it's true I want to touch them.

•

Your face is Classical, your body, Hellenistic.
Carved from two blocks, no one can be sure
you are even Venus. Found 200 years ago,
nearly 2000 years after you were born,

there is no proof you are special. If you were mine,
alive, and in the morning light
I saw you from behind, towel falling from you
like it is now, part of me would fill with love,

the other part with an intense urge to run away.
I can make of you whatever I want:
the twist of your body as the beginning of a dance,
your nudity as desire. Is that the hint of a smirk?

Only from a certain angle, and this is the power of art:
to change, to be a reflection of the viewer.
Not the artist—no one even knows who made you.
I made you. And right now you are making me.


•


Two days later, Venus, I return to you, to gaze
at your body again, to contend with the nature
of art and desire and being a man.
You remind me of how alone I am, and how

I can never make a great statement. Today your being
assaulted by photos feels even more invasive,
your privacy violated. I imagine your right arm
reaching down to pull up your gown, to become modest.

This is what I want for you: to become modest, to conquer
maleness. But still I want you, because I cannot
have you, because you are like everything
I cannot have, because this I know is not

the last time I'll think of you, because
at this moment the crowd has parted
so that I can see you clearly and only now can I see
the weary lean of your shoulders, the pain in your face.

# Notice the Hills

Notice the hills because they may not be
*natural*, the tour guide said, and pointing
she quickly moved on to say the city
was full of so much old and new it was

to die for.  The guide admitted that, yes,
horrors had occurred here, but a new day
had dawned, and tearing down is the first step
to building up, and that only great hope

could move us from strife and into glory.
Hours later, in my hotel, fruit flies
circled a fist of browning bananas.
They flew madly without pattern or plan

amidst the fading glow of fair twilight,
and were much too quick and too small to catch.
Millions of years ago the dinosaurs
died out and that too led to a greater

future, but, that night, as I watched the flies
I thought of the tour guide, how she said earth
has a way of making invisible
its deepest scars, and how men became hills.

# Good King Wenceslas

I picture him, boots in the snow
like two birds in the snow,
striding with purpose
towards his aim, on the day
of the feast of Stephen. This good king,
striding in the bluster,
wind like deep space, he went
to give food and comfort
to a poor man from a distant land
and now I for this act tear up
in an all-you-can-eat all-you-can-
drink buffet in Budapest, the Danube
like a jewel, while back in Prague
you get Wenceslas with a massive statue.
He on his statue is meters in the air
atop his royal horse,
its regal garments aglow in stone
and what are we trying to say here?
The King has his song, he is the image
of the pious king not too great
to help a stranger in the cold.
But listen to the song again.
With him in his mercy is his page,
brought along, with no agency.
And this page, his hands, his two human
hands of lower station hustled along
in the righteous vigor of his king
as the winter chill clasps his body
like a cuff, his hands, how cold
were they that night, how yearning for fire,
for freedom, for choice?

# Nostalgia for a Distant Future

When after many years I return to Mars
I find it foreign, like the taste of pineapple
or like myself in so many places
where the world shoots its bright sun
across a potato field. I didn't know
how to be alone, and so I was, like Kafka
in his early work, yearning after a woman
on a tram, a nearby flock of bats like a castle.
There was much wondering. Kafka
in his late work did this but how late
could it be, dying at 41? When you arrive
in the land of the Martians
do not worry, because they are gone now.
Likewise, Hussites who destroyed the churches
of the early Czech world – do not worry –
they are gone now. Burn all but these few,
Kafka said, and because his friends were traitors
we have his dreams. Here in 2525
the earth like Mars and air and what we drink
is red red red like some apples
when we had those. And when an asteroid
conquers your peace to offer you the best
opaque sunset, try hard to ignore it.

# Dracula's Last Day

Parliament is a dream that wakes Dracula at 3 PM.
A cold sweat, and at times like this,
the universe contracting like a universe,

we see him as a child, before the hunger for blood
became stronger than his will to innocence.
Awake—and in this version of the myth

he still sleeps when the sun
bakes the sand under your feet—he stares at the ceiling.
His heart flutters like 13 blackbirds.

He gets up and responds to some emails,
texts a girl or two he's been after, now that he's too shy
to approach them in person. But why parliament?

In his dream he imagined the tribunal
that would finally figure him out,
that would make him pay for his crimes,

his jaywalking, his riding the metro without a ticket,
his neck biting, his not showering
before using the thermal bath at Szechenyi,

his neck biting. I have been alive for so long, he says
out loud and to no one. *So long.* And then,
on his door, stake in hand, the woman knocks.

# The Italians Have It Right

Drink wine

    then drink espresso

    then drink wine

In the intermission

    art

    pasta

    sex beneath the chandelier and in the curved nape of the
    gondola

We let it move like night through its lights

    the moon a scimitar

    the stars too many

Four thousand miles away potential love awaits

    so our hero texts with near-deranged calculation


    *


In a bout of naiveté one could say the universe is a cocoon or
    husk of impermanence

    minus you

the adventurer

in a despair state throttling

So thank God in Heaven such bouts don't last

Everything that is ungood can be drowned via purchase of
haute couture Milano knockoffs cast by distant Chinese
hands

or in a canal

There are churches everywhere

The eyes of Christ are upon you

like those of Texas

and from these truths there is no escape

because at the Last Supper Judas was either made aware
of the knowledge of his own deceit

or made aware he was all along part of the plan

Asshole as martyr

Innocent as the punished

*

Before long it has been long and hope became like the
Roman amphitheater on which our hero spit to make
some point about capital

A bunch of rocks

a cistern

idealism dogged by greed or belief and it so happens the
girl didn't work out as that earlier night when our hero
cried with joy like he didn't know possible decayed

a memory now

a Roman amphitheater at which he ate an olive before it
was ready

This is the shape of regret

this is a black cat in the alleyway of black cats

black cats

black cats

This is the struggle to find parking

This is no worries if the biggest museum is missed

as it's just full of brilliance anyway

"Brilliance" from Latin

It means "to shine like a precious stone"

God

My dear

I thought you'd be someone

but I guess instead you are a colosseum of despair

Let me hold you just one more time

let me feed you to the lions

# Where You Are Going Is What You Are

*Inside this making*
                    *is the maker,*

*inside this miracle*
                    *is the miracle,*

*the billions of stars*

*who give light*
                    *to automobiles at night,*

*the moon a bowl of milk a cat stalks after—*

*where you are going*
                    *is no mystery,*

*where you are going*
                    *is what you are.*

# Forgotten

# Homecoming

When I go to pick up the easel
what is left of my dreams but another last night
in a litany of last nights? A dog
barks outside, I shout at the dog,

I shout again, and a car passes
with its headlights the burnt out eyes
of a blind pastor. Oh sightless stars
in the heavens, who cannot wonder about you

but a child who hasn't asked a question,
or an old man who has answered
all of his? His knees creak like a house
settling, a husband settling, a tree bowing

from the million birds of five dozen migrations.
When I count my gold I am like an empire,
and when has one of those lasted?
If you listen closely you can hear

the green sea below as it laps its edges
like a horse at a pond. An old woman prays
to a god of dust, her hands full of necklaces.
Meanwhile, I went home.

# My Mother Shaving Her Legs

My mother never quite knows when it's time
to get rid of things. The newspaper clipping
with a comic about a dog chewing a newspaper,
the button of her son, now grown, as a little leaguer,
the hat too large for his head, his teeth
not yet straightened by braces, the handwritten
eulogy for someone's grandmother. These things
are magneted with less than care to the refrigerator,
itself full of too much that should be gone,
and this is not all her fault. She is not alone,
she is surrounded, she is a part of an architecture
whose floor plan has grown too sprawling to control,
its rooms piled high with yesterday's treasures
and with yesterdays. There are artifacts of memory
everywhere, on every flat surface, and hanging
from things that things can be hung from.
I don't blame her. It's hard to make sense of this world.
It's hard to make sense of feeling the need
for something when there is so much already had.
That yearning, that realization that it's easier
to dream of hope than to confront the disappointment
that is what is: none of her sons want
to take out the trash, none of them want to listen.
In time all children are disappointments,
not necessarily because their careers
didn't become careers, or because the partners
they chose or who chose them didn't quite fit,
but because they don't love back the way they should.
So here she is, in the tub, or balancing
on its rail, the razor in hand, as she makes
one neat row of white after another, disappear.
It's like years, or dreams, this disappearing.

# All You Know on Earth
## and All You Need to Know

The man lay there on the board like you'd imagine a dead
man to lay

He's on the board beneath the dull lights of the funeral
home and over his body is draped a sheet

It is as if he is a body on television

but this isn't television

His face is pouring in on itself and around him in their turn
his grandsons drape their bodies over him for what has
been lost

A room over

the grandsons

look at different urns

They are different than what you'd expect

I'd pictured Keats' Grecian urn

something fantastic with pipers gaily dittying

a scene of resurrection or the ornaments of elegance

Instead the urns aren't like vases at all

They're just boxes

different kinds of boxes into which you place a man as if
he were a pair of shoes

Most of the boxes are wood and some of them advertise
    their impermeability

    that they will protect the dead man from the elements

    that he will remain in his little prison forever

Nothing gets in

    nothing gets out

Let's get a drink

    says the father

    and unlike when his mother died two years earlier

    this time we won't have to listen to his uncomfortable
    spastic sobs while everyone else is trying to have a good
    time

He has five sons and no one knows how to comfort anyone

It's not natural for these men

    this hugging and consolation thing

It feels weak

As all of this is happening the man is still there

On the board

# Oblique Letter to Young Son
as He Confronts Adolescent Loneliness
for the First Time

When the water is all around you
you know you are the land, son.

Unlike your surroundings
only your tears and soul are wet,

the rest of you a buoy
flicked like a pistachio shell

into the merciless eons of outer space.
The sun is still a ball of fire,

it is the high-efficiency bulb
of God, by which he writes his songs

and crucifies his child. But
let's not be bleak; you, son,

are the land, the firmament
filled with surprise, like a girl

out of whose hand a giraffe's tongue
grabs a snack. In this mystery

we get only so many chances to live,
to fight off the last breath

and pay our taxes just one more time.
When the body is an ark

all the animals are in you
and you can call it what you want –

salvation, damnation,
another day at the mercy of the tides.

# Sick Child as Hailstorm

There is nothing like a sick kid
The boiling furnace of a small body

The sweat of it
Pathetic like lightning

Whose thunder you can't hear
A little mystery of love

The child's hands reaching out
The cup of chicken noodle shaking

When the child is like this
My love is too much to bear

The hail hits the lawn
It rips through the trees

Every surface of nature is pummeled
It is like a coyote

A coyote carrying a rabbit
I can't hear the thunder

I can only hear what is breaking
I put a cold cloth on the child's forehead

There is no reconciling
The sacred with the self

The profound paling
Beneath this fever this child

The hail piles up
It is piling up on all our bodies

It is too much to bear
This love

# Apples

What am I supposed to do
with the glorious wreckage
of a burnt out police car
or heart except cheer?
To travel the world is one thing
and to travel the mind
is the same thing so nothing
really changed no matter
the continents crisscrossed
as this grassless backyard
is the same royal nothing
as any other rest of the world
vast as hereditary injustice
in which people should wear
masks but often don't.
And what of it but my children
still here stunting daily
in their underdevelopments
like unwatered wildflowers
as the school is shuttered
and would you believe
it was named after Robert E. Lee
and what twenty thirty
years from now will the kids
make of the shapeless weekdays
or the cumulus of teargas
gesturing across the interstate?
The time to wander prodigal
may be over but I'll wonder
where wandering led. I'll say
I've always been here, watching.
My fear is a sparrow
who trembles in a thunderstorm.
All foolish kings hoard

what they want to hoard.
I'll lock and deadbolt the door
and while the fires of correction
raze the wicked architecture
of so many centuries' cruelty
I'll try to raise my children
to be sweet like an orchard.

# The Next Generation

If the child says *I am bored*
I say do you want the hatchet

Of course the child wants the hatchet
The child says *where is it*

You can find it in the garage
I say I will not help you find it

It is in the dark place of the garage
Look for the dark place and there you will find the hatchet

It is with the spiders
Go where the spiders are I say

And then a miracle occurs
This is the miracle

The hatchet glinting its glint in the noontime sun
The child learns to use it

He uses it well
He wields it like a dream of peace between the factions of
    stubborn nations

And this is how I show my love
My love is too large

All night and all day I think of love
I think of the child my child

In the backyard standing
Next to the tree that used to be our Christmas tree

I see him there
And in his hand his strong small strong weak child's hand

Raised high
The hatchet

# We Cannot Leave the House

I played Parcheesi yesterday
Yahtzee today
Don't know how long I can keep that up
Been reading a lot too    brutal
I watch the exponential growth curve
I see all the articles with their scary math
And know again like a child that math is scary
I'm here with my kids in our bubble
And how long before they get tired of fruit snacks
And turn to me to fill their bellies
It's okay it's what I'm here for
To grow their inheritance
To make a nest of time and string like a bird
As the walls close in
Oh those children    oh the hot crisis
Of the stock market and climate
Their love their endless love
And what is it to be a father but to be present
But to be the absence of absence
The pancake-making blade that hovers
Above their futures    these boys
With their blue-eyed devilry
The imperial bliss of their livingroom fortbuilding
The underweared consumption of ice cream
Like weekends are not ends
Because here as we wait for the virus
I lift this house by my shoulders
And here as we wait for the virus    so pretty
We are family
And here as we wait for the virus
Soon the world's manic hoarding will end
and the using will begin

# When at the End of One Thing
# and at the Beginning of Another

Wind does not breathe. It is the breath,
and every night is a meteor, where I scroll

through the history of universes and my grandmother
like an archaeologist of hope. Here we are,

my little desperate heart-filled heart of blood,
watch how it seeks new ways to turn emotions

into emojis. Like a blind man looking at a phone
I make sense of absence, and imagine all


Neruda deleted from his poems, how he said
to write well you must know how to delete

and that's why I met him on a snow-covered precipice
where he pushed me off so I could learn

my wings were ready. I would rather die
600 medieval deaths than try to sew shut the pockets

my money has been burning through,
because ending this dance without debt


is a wasted chance to win: all failure
is preceded by potential, just like the flower

before it blooms. The flower needs no blooming
to have been a flower and night's awakening into day

isn't a blunder but just the fluttering of lashes
as light shines through the blinds.

Time is always wandering the quilt of earth
because it is a collage and your eyes are the museum,


so I tried to read unwritten pages as always
and that's why I looked through the screen

to see the screen I was seen through. In Latvia
I bought caviar in a converted Nazi zeppelin hangar

and my life has become about collecting sentences
like this. Once in Cuba I met a Russian psychotherapist

and gave her the blueprints she sought
in exchange for keys to a door I couldn't find,


and on Good Friday I couldn't help but accidentally
say Jesus in response to things large and small

and every time I did I felt him there, saving.
Or did I? A leaf in summer resists interpretation

unlike its fall and spring counterparts
but where does that leave the leaf in winter?

This is why I make the fanciest drink to feel
as if glowing the hours away is the way to glow.


When at the end of one thing and at the beginning
of another I discover how a cell membrane

is an illusion, how not celebrating a death
is like mourning a life: it betrays

a misunderstanding of how this whole show works.
When huddled cross-legged beside a tree

by yourself and in a trance you don't need
to intend for your heart to beat for it to beat.


But this is real life, and if it is smiling I will love it,
because in America we trust in pragmatism,

our sole contribution to philosophy, even if
it is a weak-minded and simplistic philosophy.

It is all we have: wind does not breathe. It is the breath.
That's intense, my eldest child says.

So I ask him to help me write a poem for this girl I like.
Aye yai yai, he says, returning to his Cheerios.

# Conclusion

The more I learn what I am not
the more I learn what I am. The more I learn what I am
the more I learn what I can never be.
This is the problem with being American:
we are just so young, we have learned nothing.
I would say I wish I could start it all
all over again, but I don't.
At the end of life will I feel I did enough?
Will I visit the moon and say, eh, I've seen this?
How can anything be awesome if the awe is over?
There still is so much more to do, and maybe someday
I will be more than a staggering fool.
Maybe I will be a better person.
Maybe I'll learn to relax. Whether it be
through France or Hungary or the Netherlands
or through Ecuador and Peru, or breathing the sun
in Kenya or Morocco or taking train after train
after train across the complicated alternative reality
that is Japan, Emerson, despite his many flaws,
was right: no matter where you run you cannot run
from yourself. So hold on, because the car
you're riding in is the only car you have.
Tolerate yourself. Enjoy the world of things.
Love your children because they really are all you have.

# To Keep Us Warm

The forgotten world
is not coming back,
not when love is there
in bed, too dark to see
but there, simmering.
The body of another
is the hot life of a galaxy
in a form even a child
can understand.
On a future copper
evening, help
those who need help.
There used to be a lot
out there but now
there's a lot in here:
a spoon clacking
the bowl as a dog
laps the soup, a spiral
of bubbles down the bath.
A bird who does not fledge.
The ceiling fan curling
its petals like a flower
is a flower and the flower
is talking all night long.
It is keeping me up.
There are all these years
left to try to live, so
what. Spiritually, memory
is a sand dune
on an unseasonably cool
summer night.
Can we reclaim the lost?
Do we need a fire?

# Acknowledgments

First, thank you to you for reading this book. It is a privilege and honor to be read.

Second, all author proceeds from the sale of this book are donated to the below-listed charities. If you have bought this book and would like to earmark your purchase for a particular charity listed, please reach out. It's always nice to have a real person behind the contribution:

> Seed School Kibera, a nonprofit serving children in the Kibera informal settlement in Nairobi, Kenya
>
> NAACP Legal Defense and Educational Fund, advocating for fair treatment for Blacks in the American justice system
>
> The National Alliance to End Homelessness, combating poverty and supporting positive urban initiatives
>
> World Wide Fund for Nature, working for wilderness preservation and the protection of species.

Thank you to *Harvard Review*, *AGNI*, *Salamander*, *Gulf Coast*, *Sixth Finch*, *The Banyan Review*, *Forklift, Ohio* and *Action, Spectacle* for having published poems—often with different forms and titles—from this collection.

Thank you to Kyle McCord and the rest of the Gold Wake Press family for their support and friendship. Thank you to Trey Moody for trying to save me. Thank you to Rashad, Andrew, Kim, and Finny for always being there. Thank you to my siblings and parents for making me who I am. Thank you to my children Will and Sam for keeping it loud and thank you to my love, Lisa, for being my sweet beauty.

# About Nick Courtright

Nick Courtright is the author of *Let There Be Light* and *Punchline*, and is the Executive Editor of Atmosphere Press. His work has appeared in *The Harvard Review*, *Kenyon Review*, and *The Southern Review*, among dozens of others. With a Doctorate in Literature from the University of Texas, Nick lives in Austin with the poet Lisa Mottolo and their children, William and Samuel.

Find him at atmospherepress.com, nickcourtright.com, and watching birds on his porch.